# First World War
## and Army of Occupation
# War Diary
## France, Belgium and Germany

27 DIVISION
Divisional Troops
Divisional Cyclist Company
1 January 1915 - 1 November 1915

WO95/2257/2

The Naval & Military Press Ltd
www.nmarchive.com
Published in association with The National Archives

Published by

## The Naval & Military Press Ltd

Unit 10 Ridgewood Industrial Park,

Uckfield, East Sussex,

TN22 5QE England

Tel: +44 (0) 1825 749494

www.naval-military-press.com

www.nmarchive.com

*This diary has been reprinted in facsimile from the original. Any imperfections are inevitably reproduced and the quality may fall short of modern type and cartographic standards.*

© **Crown Copyright**
**Images reproduced by permission of The National Archives, London, England, 2015.**

# Contents

| Document type | Place/Title | Date From | Date To |
|---|---|---|---|
| Heading | WO95/2257/2 | | |
| Heading | 27th Division Divl Troops 27th Divl Cyclist Company Dec 1914-Nov 1915 | | |
| War Diary | | 21/12/1915 | 31/12/1915 |
| War Diary | | 01/01/1915 | 01/11/1915 |

W095/22547/2

**27TH DIVISION**
**DIVL TROOPS**

27TH DIVL CYCLIST COMPANY
DEC 1914 - NOV 1915

27TH DIVISION
DIVL TROOPS

# 27 CYCLISTS

Dec '14
(6
Nov '15)

**Page 2**

| Date | |
|---|---|
| 21st December | Embarked on S.S. ARCHITECT at SOUTHAMPTON, embarkation completed by 3.30 p.m. Total Strength 8 Officers & 202 other ranks, 210 bicycles, 2 G.S. Wagons, 1 limbered wagon, 4 Heavy Draught Horses & 2 light draught horses. Sailed at 8 p.m. |
| 22nd December | Arrived HAVRE at daybreak. Disembarked men & machines at 10 a.m. Wagons & horses 4 p.m. Delay caused by own wagons being in rear of hold & G.S.E. wagons having to be removed first. Billeted in large shed in docks. |
| 23rd December | Marched to Goods Station & entrained. Bicycles placed in rows across large open flat wagon trucks. About 60 to a truck. Cord was sewn to hold in place & outside machines had handle bars lashed, to avoid any projection beyond side of truck. Men accommodated in covered vans with sliding doors, one platoon to a truck i.e. about 31 men. Officers in two first class compartments. Major Calverly Surrey Yeomanry in command of train. |
| 24th December | Arrived ARQUES detrained at 10 a.m. Bicycles received no damage & method of packing proved satisfactory. Proceeded to billets at village of LYNDE |

**Page 3**

| | |
|---|---|
| | Nos 3 & 4 Platoons, Transport & Company H.Q. in Brasserie. Nos 1, 2, 5 & 6 Platoons in Farms & houses in village. |
| 25th Dec: | Inspection and overhaul of machines, rifles equipment and clothing. Lecture to Officers " " N.C.Os. |
| 26th Dec: | Reported arrival of company to General Staff 27th Div; at ARQUES. Platoons covered under Platoon Cmdrs. Company Parade at 2 p.m. March discipline and naming of orders. Field telephone laid from 80th Inf: Bde H.Qrs to Cyclist H.Qrs. No 9356 L Cpl Blunt
" 9137 " Hogan } 27 Glo: Regt Equipt & Despatch
" 8306 " Hayter } as above
Company Parade, advance guards No 1 & 2 Platoons to HAZEBROUCK. Dinners out. |
| 27th Dec: | Nos 3 & 4 advance guard on return. Riding and march discipline improving. Voluntary Church Parade at 8 a.m. for R.Cs. 30 men present. |
| 28th Dec: | Company parade, advance guards to AIRE. Dinners out. Platoons moved back by different routes. |

WAR DIARY 27 CYCLISTS Army Form C. 2118.

4

Great improvement. Passing of orders still poor.

29th Dec: Patrols & concentration on CASSEL
Dinners out.
Return to billets by double platoons.
Patrols fairly satisfactory, N.C.Os require more instruction in Map Reading.

30th Dec Patrol scheme South of AIRE.
Dinners out.
Platoons returned independantly.
Despatch riding very bad. Patrols show great improvement & Patrol leaders more initiative.
Baths arranged for men in Brasserie.
Each platoon allotted a distinctive coloured band for their machines.
Officers platoon band & one white band.

~~31st Dec~~
31st Dec Despatch riding (3 lines) from LYNDE to Marie at HARZEBROUCK.
All lines worked well & messages passed in both directions very quickly inspite of head winds & bad roads.
Concentrated at HARZEBROUCK.
Dinners out.
Platoons returned independantly by different routes.

1915

**1st Jan:** Company Parade & attack scheme round SERCUS.
Platoons worked except No 6 which was badly led & commanded.
Alarm given at night about midnight. On investigation proved to be men of R.P.C.L.I. firing rifles up in church.
Reported again to 80th Bde Hd Qrs.
No 10090 Pte Gleeson awarded 8 days F.P. No 1 for absence without leave.

**2nd Jan:** Platoons under platoon sergeants.
Scouts & observers under officers.
No 10586 Pte Ramsey R. Scots awarded 5 days No 2I for absence.
Platoons under platoon cmdrs.

**3rd Jan:** Company inspection of cycles & uniforms.

**4th Jan:** Advance guard & attack scheme to SI VENANT under Capt Green.
Proceeded to 80th Bde Hd Qrs for orders re move from present billets.
Recalled company & proceeded to pack up.

**5th Jan:** Paraded 8.30 a.m. No 4 platoon, advance guard. Transport parade 7.45 a.m.
First Halt HARZEBROUCK.
Reported to G.O.C. 2nd Army, who examined bicycles etc.
Arrived METEREN 12 noon.
No casualties.

Company billeted in Communal School.
Reported arrival to Hd Qrs 80th Inf Bde.
Received orders to proceed to BOESCHEPE.

**6th Jan:** Paraded 9.30 a.m.
Arrived BOESCHEPE 12 noon.
No casualties.
1 man R. Scots admitted to Hospital from METEREN.
Nos 1 & 2 Platoons billeted in one Farm.
Nos 3, 4, 5 & 6 Platoons, Coy Hd Qrs & Transport billeted in another Farm.
Farms in very insanitary condition.
Whole company occupied cleaning up & erecting & digging latrines.
Washing rooms etc, inspection of machines.
Reported to 27th Div: Hd: Qrs.

**7th Jan:** Platoons under platoon Cmdrs. Coy paraded at 2.p.m. Inspection of bicycles of whole company.

**8th Jan:** Orders received to patrol two field telephone lines running from D.H.Q. to DICKEBUSCH.
No 1 & 2 platoons perf. relief.
No 10657 L-Cpl Dewar 2/R.9. R. deprived of Lance Stripe.
No 10253-12th Wade 2/R.9. Rgt appointed L-Cpl vice Dewar.

**9th Jan:** Orders received to train one officer & NCOs & 36 men as bomb throwers for enemy trench

27 CYCLISTS

11th Jan: Mills & Rifle Grenades.
Selected Lt Otway to command party under instruction.
Visited No 2 line patrols & found all correct.

12th Jan: Belgian arrested for starting wire of shirt off R.S.L. 9 wagon, handed him over to A.P.M. 27th Division. Visited No 1 line.
Arranged for Surrey Yeomanry to assist in patrolling. One platoon were able to carry out patrolling.
Got into touch with 3rd Division Cyclist Coy.

13th Jan: Visited 1 & 2 lines & DICKEBUSCH.
Patrols working satisfactorily with one platoon.

14th Jan: Road report of all roads to POPERINGHE.
Visited some suspected farms at night with A.P.M. Arranged baths for Company.

15th Jan: Coy Sergt Major Dunham admitted to hospital. Sergt Witts No 4 Platoon appointed a/Coy Sergt Major.
Road reports to RENINGHELST.

16th Jan: 1 N.C.O. & 8 men of Bomb throwing party sent to DICKEBUSCH, also 10 men as Dispatch riders.
Spent night watching for signalling.
Patrols report all clear.

17th Jan: —

18th Jan: Received 4 new R.S.A. machines from A.O.D.
Road reports to BAIZEUL.
Patrols report all clear.

19th Jan: Patrols report all clear.
Road reports OVERDOM district.

20th Jan: Field General Court Martial assembled at Company Hd Qrs for trial of No 8768 Pte Lawler 1/R.I. Regt.
Redistribution of men of Company. No 6 Platoon formed of Bomb Throwers only.

No 8973 L/Cpl Caulfield 2/Leinster Regt appointed Lance sergt.
No 8857 Pte Wynhows 2/Leinster Regt appointed Lance corporal vice Caulfield.

21st Jan: Relief of Bomb Throwers sent to DICKEBUSCH also dispatch riders.
Road reports MINOIR district.

22nd Jan: Order received no lights allowed to show towards the front from 8pm to dawn.
Road reports VLAMATINGHE district.

23rd Jan: Company Parade & usual patrols
24th Jan: No 24973 Pte Gillespie 1/R.I. Regt myoits 10 days/pay for absence.
No 8762 Pte Lawler 1/R.I. Regt awarded one months F.P. No 1 by Field General Court Martial. Only promulgated before company.

24th Jan: 1 Trench mortar burst in trenches, 2 PPCLI killed, 2 wounded.

25th Jan: Bomb throwers wiring rifle grenades checked work in German Sap.

26th Jan: Handed in completed Road reports & usual patrols.

27th Jan: Company parade & usual patrols.

**WAR DIARY**
or
**INTELLIGENCE SUMMARY.**

Army Form C. 2118.

**27 CYCLISTS**

9

28th Jan: Usual patrols.

29th Jan: Relief for bomb throwers & despatch riders sent up to DICKEBUSCH.

30th Jan: No SP 08 L-Cpl Vaughan 1/Lincoln Rgt. killed upon entering No 9 trench at 7.30.a.m. 27th Div: 1/Lincoln Rgt. & 3rd Echelon Base duly notified.

31st Jan: Usual patrols

**Army Form C. 2118.**

# WAR DIARY or INTELLIGENCE SUMMARY.

**27 CYCLISTS**

| Date | Summary of Events and Information |
|---|---|
| 1st Feb: | Usual patrol |
| 2nd Feb | Road reports VLAMERTINGE district |
| 3rd Feb | Proceeded to 27th Div: HQ RENINGHELST & arranged with O.C. 1/R.I. Fusiliers for relief. |
| 4th Feb | Sent up relief of bomb throwers & despatch riders to DICKEBUSCH also Lt SHAFTO in relief of Lt OTWAY. Company parade & march to BAILLEUL & return. |
| 5th Feb | 2Lt Morgan promoted Lieut (London Gazette 28/1/15) |
| 6th Feb | No 2 Platoon on patrol in relief of No 3 Platoon. |
| 7th Feb | No 5 Platoon on patrol in relief of No 2 Platoon. |
| 8th Feb | No 1 Platoon on patrol in relief of No 5 Platoon. |
| 9th Feb | No 2 Platoon on patrol in relief of No 1 Platoon. No 9069 Pte W. Heavy 1/Lunster Regt struck off strength. |
| 10th Feb | Field General C.M. on No 4913 Pte Gillespie 2/R.I.F. Lts Lyne & Vyvyan members. No 3 Platoon on patrol |
| 11th Feb | No 4 Platoon on patrol. |
| 12th Feb | No 5 Platoon on patrol. |
| 13th Feb | No 1 Platoon on patrol. |
| 14th Feb | Company moved to WESTOUTRE. Billeted in Convent. No 3 on Patrol. |
| 15th Feb | Company returned to BOESCHEPE 1pm. Sent up Lt Otway & relief of Bomb Throwers to DICKEBUSCH. |
| 16th Feb | No 1 & 2 Platoons moved into Coy Hd Qrs billet. Relief of bomb throwing party. |
| 17th Feb | Company moved to RENINGHELST arrived 12.40p.m. Billeted in Farm |
| 18th Feb | Company returned to BOESCHEPE |
| 19th Feb | Usual patrols. No 10979 Pte McGill & No 10719 Pte Malone 2/R.I. Fusiliers awarded 14 days F.P. No 1, for absence. |
| 20th Feb | Usual patrols |
| 21st Feb | Company parade. |
| 22nd Feb | No 10760 Pte Turbett killed in action 21/2/15 |
| 23rd Feb | Company parade. |

Army Form C. 2118.

27 C. LISTE

# WAR DIARY
or
## INTELLIGENCE SUMMARY.
(Erase heading not required.)

Instructions regarding War Diaries and Intelligence Summaries are contained in F. S. Regs., Part II. and the Staff Manual respectively. Title pages will be prepared in manuscript.

| Place | Date | Hour | Summary of Events and Information | Remarks and references to Appendices |
|---|---|---|---|---|

11

24th Feb — Usual patrols

25th Feb — F.G. Crank Invalided on N° 10846 Pte Scots.

26th Feb — N° 8646 Pte H. Tandy died from wounds.

27th Feb — Company Parade.

28th Feb — N° 11073 Pte Chapman 2/R.? Fusiliers 14 days F.P.N°1 for "Drunkenness & Leaving his billet without permission."

(10346) W: W5300/P713 750,000 3/18 E 2688 Forms/C2118/16.

# WAR DIARY
## or
## INTELLIGENCE SUMMARY.
(Erase heading not required.)

Army Form C. 2118.

27 CYCLISTS

| Place | Date | Hour | Summary of Events and Information | Remarks and references to Appendices |
|---|---|---|---|---|
| | 1st March | | No 0845 Pte J Graham 1/R Scotts sentenced by F.G.C.M to 6 mths H.L./pc drunkenness commuted to 2 months F.P. No 2. | |
| | 2nd March | | Lt Wynyan 2/1 S.L.I & No 10058 P.S.T. Hall killed in action. No 1 Platoon Lunchoft duty for bomb throwing | |
| | 3rd March | | Proceeded to DICKEBUSCH to inspect bomb throwers & dispatch riders, arranged about disposal of Lt Wynyans Kit. | |
| | 4th March | | Usual patrols | |
| | 5th March | | Usual patrols | |
| | 6th March | | Lt Pyne to DICKEBUSCH in charge of bomb throwers. | |
| | 7th March | | No 6 Platoon relieved No 3 Platoon on patrol. Relief of despatch riders at DICKEBUSCH. | |
| | 8th March | | Usual patrols. | |
| | 9th March | | Proceeded to RENINGHELST inspected billets of No 3 Platoon & verified roads between RENINGHELST & VLARMATINGH#. | |

Army Form C. 2118.

## 27 CYCLISTS SUMMARY

| Date | Events and Information |
|---|---|
| 10th March | No. 10916 L/Cpl McArthur A.C.C. deprived of 2nd Stripe for drunkenness. No. 9235 Pte Pennyfather/Pimlico 14 days No. 1 F.P. for drunkenness |
| 11th March | No. 1 Platoon moved to DICKEBUSCH in relief of No. 6. |
| 12th March | No. 10829 Pte Anderson A.C.C. 14 days No. 2 F.P. & deprived of 2 days pay for absence. Usual patrols & platoon parades. No. 2 & 3 Platoons under bomb throwing instruction. |
| 13th March | Proceeded to RENINGHELST, attended at now. Hot qrs, also 8 O.M. Pte Holspin signaling bomb throwing instruction. |
| 14th March | Received order to "Stand to" 6.15 p.m. Extremely heavy cannonading along left of 2nd Div: No. 5 Platoon changed billets |
| 15th March | Standing to. Casualties:- No. 21839 2nd Cpl Simmons & 9003 Pte Finucan missing. No. 2333 - No. 2 Hewitt & No. 9882 Pte Holland wounded. |
| 16th March | Received news. Pte Finucan now reported wounded. |
| 17th March | No. 1 Platoon moved to DICKEBOSCH in relief of No. 6. Usual patrols & platoon parades. |
| 18th March | Lt Pyne reported sick. Lieut Penny took charge of No. 3 & 4 platoons & Lt Otway i/c No. 1 & 6 Platoons. |
| 19th March | Visited No. 5 Platoon also on patrol |
| 20th March | Platoon parades & patrols. Usual patrols |
| 21st March | Usual patrols. O.C. 3rd Div. Nil Troops visited Coy HQ prior to impending moves in name. |
| 22nd March | Proceeded to RENINGHELST visited patrols. LtCpl. 13 proceeded on 14 days sick leave to England. |
| 23rd March | Proceeded to Divl Qrs at trench mortars to Brigadiers relief by 3rd Div. |
| 24th March | Stored surplus bicycles in loft of Mr Runts cottage. Communicated with 3rd Div. Cyclists regarding wire patrol relief. |
| 25th March | Company parade. Company in attack |
| 26th March | Company parade. Company in attack |
| 27th March | Platoon parade, march discipline. |
| 28th March | Company parade, road patrols. Night march |
| 29th March | Platoon parade, road patrols |
| 30th March | Company parade. outpost work picketing |
| 31st March | Company parade. road picketing |

**27 CYCLIST**
**April 1915**

**WAR DIARY**
Army Form C. 2118.

| Date | Entry |
|---|---|
| 1st April | Platoon parade, map reading |
| 2nd April | Company parade, enemy tactical points (railway) |
| 3rd April | Received orders to move. |
| 4th April | Moved to new billets at YPRES. Arrived 4.15 pm. Relieved No 5 Platoon on wire patrols. |
| 5th April | Lt Lyne rejoined from sick leave. Reported to Div Hd Qrs |
| 6th April | Moved to permanent billet in Ecole Moyenne RUE DE LA BOURSE. Sent up Lts Renny & Lyne to select trench mortar positions. |
| 7th April | Platoon parade, wire patrols |
| 8 " | [brought in wire cages in case of attack] |
| 9 " | [men for bomb throwing Lt Lyne in charge] |
| 10 " | Coy parade |
| 11 " | Wire patrol Plt 7 26 men |
| 12 " | Given to R.P.M. for traffic control |
| 13 " | Major General Snow inspected billet & cellars |
| 14 " | Coy ordered to stand by (not called out) |
| 15 " | Coy standing by (not called out) |
| 16 " | |
| 17 " | Capt Adams proceeded on 5 days leave, Capt Hilton-Green assumed command. |
| 18 " | Coy called out to clear roads for traffic near Menin Bridge. Lt Morgan admitted to hospital. |
| 19 " | Lt Shafto to hospital. Coy ordered to bivouack in field. squad No 6 or |
| 20 " | Coy employed on making dugouts |
| 21 " | Major General Snow visited camp, warned Coy regarding aeroplane reconnaissance. draft of officers not for No 22 on arrival. |
| 22 " | Capt Adams returned from leave & assumed command. Coy called out to report to Adv S.H.Q. arrived at S.H.Q. 8.20 pm. Ordered to send reconnoitring patrols to trenches of 28th Divn & report position & happenings |

14

April 1915

8th. Billeted in the school in Rue de la Bouche YPRES. Engaged on clearing the cellars to make cover from shell fire.

9th. N.C.O. & 5 men for bomb throwing — Lieut Lyon in charge.

10th. Company parade for instruction map-reading etc.

11th. Wire patrol N.C.O. & 20 men.

12th. 6 men to A.P.M. for traffic control

13th. Major-General Snow, Y.O. Snow, Y.O.B. 27th Division inspected billets & cellars, commended C.O. on precautions taken in clearing cellars.

14th. Occasional shells on Ypres from enemy's guns. Coy ordered to stand by, but was not called out.

15th. Coy "standing by," was not called out.

16th. "          "          "          "

17th. Coy reverted to normal state of readiness. Capt Adams proceeded on 5 days leave. Capt H.J.L. Hilton-Green assumed command.

18th. Coy called out to clear roads for traffic near MENIN Bridge, road was strewed with bricks mortar etc owing to heavy bombardment with shells of large calibre, Lt Morgan admitted to hospital.

19th. Lieut Shafto to hospital, Coy ordered to leave the town owing to heavy bombardment. Bivouacked in square H.6.a.

20th. Coy employed on making bivouacs

21st. Major-General Snow visited camp & warned Coy about Aeroplane reconnaissance & taking all available cover from view. Lt Robinson & 22 Other ranks arrived.

22nd. Capt Adams returned from leave & assumed command. Coy called out to Div S.H.Q (here was the commencement of the "2nd Battle of Ypres" arrived at S.H.Q at 8.20 P.M. Ordered to send reconnoitring patrols to trenches & 28th Divn (St. Julien) and report position & happenings to D.H.Q British Columbians in trenches fell back & reported enemy were using poisonous gas. Position very critical. Reported at 11.45 P.M. reinforcements urgently required.

23rd. At 1.A.M. Coy Hd. Qrs retired from WEILTJE to ST JEAN owing to heavy bombardment. Reserve Bde of 27th Divn seen on road to reinforce 28th Divn front. 11am enemy starting shelling ST JEAN. Coy retired to bivouacs Capt Adams admitted to hospital. Coy ordered out again. Capt H.J.L.

# WAR DIARY
## or
## INTELLIGENCE SUMMARY

Army Form C. 2118.

Cont:-

23rd Lt. Leary in command. Reported to Adv. B/H Qrs ordered to take up patrol work again. Position reported very critical. Coy HQrs at ST JAN

24th At 10.30 a.m. patrol reported large numbers of French reinforcements seen on YPRES - BOESINGHE RD - later two battalions of British troops on YPRES - ST JULIEN RD as reinforcements for 28th Divn front. Casualties for the day 2 men wounded.

25th Situation reported quieter. Canadians seen digging themselves in south of wood on left of ST JULIEN RD & adjoining fields. Heavy shelling all day on YPRES - ST JULIEN RD & adjoining fields. Casualties for the day 1 man wounded.

26th Heavy cannonading reported at WIELTJE - later village reported practically destroyed by enemy fire; at 1.30 p.m. enemy commenced shelling ST JAN. Coy ordered out into the fields - received message to concentrate at Adv. B.H.Q. Arrived B.H.Q. 2.45 p.m. Sent out patrols - Casualties for the day 2 men wounded.

27th Nothing important excepting arrival of British troops to reinforce 28th Divn front. Casualties for the day 1 man wounded.

28th 3rd Lahore Divn arrived & established H.Qrs in wood adjoining 24th & H.Qrs - later patrol reported that troops of 3rd Lahore Divn had taken 1st line enemy trenches near ST JULIEN - FORTUNA - Patrol reported that an enemy Aeroplane was brought down by Infantry.

28th Pilot was captured & observer killed - later Pilot cont'd brought in to 24th Fd. Ambs. Casualties for the day 2 men wounded & sent L'troy slightly wounded but was able to carry on.

29th Patrol reported that majority of lost ground had been retaken & situation quieter. Terrific shelling on the wood where our H.Qrs were situated, but no casualties.

30th Instructions issued that 1 Officer and 1 Platoon were to remain as patrol. Remainder to return to camp. This practically signified the finish of the enemies first big offensive for a long time - vide daily papers - details this battle as 2nd Battle for YPRES. Advanced B.H.Qrs moved to point on FLAMERTINGHE - OUDERDAM RD. Coy arrived in camp at 6-15 p.m. Casualties for the day, 1 man killed (Pte Ryan) and 1 man wounded

**WAR DIARY** or **INTELLIGENCE SUMMARY**

May 1915 — 1/1 CYCLISTS

Army Form C. 2118.

1st May 1915.
No. 5 & 6 platoons sent to relief Lieut Lyne and platoon on patrol, patrols reported that they expected an attack on British front. Situation remained quiet for a while. Enemy then commencing shelling heavily about 4 Pm & an enemy infantry attack was started about 5 Pm & continued till 6 Pm, with no material loss to ourselves, the enemy's attack proved unsuccessful. No casualties in this Coy.

2nd Nos 1 & 2 platoons sent in relief of 5 & 6 no casualties

3rd Coy moved to pt. near Adv. D.H.Q. No casualties.

May 1915.
4th Coy commended for work done period 22/4/15 to 30/4/15.

5th Wire patrols, Bridge Guards, Reconnoitring.

6th Party 1 N.C.O. & 5 men sent to 62nd Bde - trench - mortars.

7th Usual patrols. Lt Lyne & 2 men for trench-mortar

8th " " Coy paraded for trench digging near 1st line trenches. No casualties.

9th Usual patrols. Trench digging at night. No casualties

10th Two men Privates Darlington & Smith with Lt Lyne's trench-mortar party killed by shrapnel. Trench digging, wire patrols, bridge guards.

11th Patrols reported all front normal. Coy paraded 6 Pm for trench digging. Casualties 4 men wounded

12th Usual patrols. Nothing important reported. Coy paraded for trench digging. No Casualties.

13th Usual patrols. No Casualties.

14th " " Trench digging. No Casualties.

15th Received news of big French success near ARRAS. Usual patrols. Situation on front normal. No casualties

16th Usual patrols, Bridge Guards, Hd Qrs Guard. No casualties

17th Usual patrols, Bridge Guard. Hd Qrs Guard. No casualties

18th Orders received to move to billet on POPERINGHE - RENINGHELST Rd. Billet found to be dirty & inconvenient for this Coy. Asked owners of farm to open out house which was locked, but they refused, but they refused on being threatened they decided

27  CYCLISTS

| | |
|---|---|
| MAY 18th contd | to open. Place was found to contain Government Rations. A.P.M. was sent for & the matter was arranged. Outhouse was utilised as Q.M. stores |
| 19th | Capt Hilton-Green Commdg Boy proceeded on 5 days leave. Boy resting. |
| 20th | Lieut Shafto in command. Boy resting. Nothing important happened. |
| 21st | Terrific bombardment on front this Boy has just left. The Boy were resting some 3 to 4 miles. But the gas the enemy were using had a stinging effect on the eyes even at that distance. Boy ordered to stand by & send patrol out - patrol reported as follows :- 4th R.B. and 3rd K.R.R.C. ordered into fire trenches, remainder of this Bde.(4th KRRC & 1st KSLI) in support. Original operation orders to this Bde. were not carried out as they had to halt on Rd FLAMERTINGHE-YPRES, as the enemy were using gas on a large scale. Further orders issued to this Bde.(80th) that they were to counter-attack at the first opportunity - this was started but owing to gas again it was not completed; this was the description given by a corporal of 4th R.B. who took part in the attempted counter-attack :- KSLI were on our left, 3rd & 4th KRRG on our right flank, there was a thick hedge on our right flank when we arrived |

| | |
|---|---|
| May 20th contd | end of the hedge our man a right wheel. When marched a ½ mile - left turn, halt. Our position now was facing the enemy with the thick hedge behind us. On looking round I found that there was a gap in the hedge when it would be possible to get through his gap & cause a lot of turn as Happened his gap got a lot of turn as it seems rationally nearly everybody and when the enemy started using gas again the order was given to retire and everybody made for the "gap". when they were seen by the enemy his machine guns were turned on this gap which proved a regular trap. It was thought on reviewing the situation afterwards that the gap must have been made purposely or in any case it was not always advisable to take the easiest route when retiring. Lieut D.R. Ireland arrived the next day. Everything normal. Patrols had nothing to report. |
| May 22nd | |
| May 23 | Arrival of Lieut W.R. Wakefield and twenty five other ranks |
| May 24th | Usual patrols. Nothing to report |
| May 25th | Any reverted to ordinary state of readiness. Nothing to report |

# WAR DIARY or INTELLIGENCE SUMMARY

**Army Form C. 2118.**

**27 CYCLISTS**

May
26 Capt Sutton-Green returned from leave and
    assumed Command of Company.
    Acting Coy S/M Potts promoted to
    Colour-Serjeant and appointed Company
    Serjeant-Major (W.O. Class II)
27 } 
28 } Coy resting.
29 18 men arrived from hospital to duty
    this made strength of Coy 8 officers 196 O.R.
30th Orders received to move to new front
    and take over billets from 8th Div Cyclist
    Coy. Everything was carried out smoothly
    and on arrival billets was found to consist
    of 3 separate farms which was named
    A.B.+C. Coy employed in cleaning billets.
31st

June

1st — Coy employed on improving & cleaning billets. Usual parades etc.
2nd — See print June
3rd — do —
4th French mortar party 1 officer 8 O.R. sent to trenches. Usual guards etc:
5th Bridge guard at ERQUINGHEM started on this day. Usual patrols etc:
6th Patrol sent to try & discover horses that had stampeded from billet that had

(6th contd)

been shelled by enemy. No casualties. Usual guards etc:
7th Carried out swimming test in Canal running between the billets. Majority of Coy good swimmers. L/Cpl Lawrence wounded. Usual guards etc:
8th Usual parades and guards.
9th Orders issued all ranks must carry respirators on person. Usual parades etc
10th Short leave to England started this day. Nothing else to report.
11th to 15th } Usual guards, patrols, training etc
16th Pte Haughy of this Coy awarded 1 yr. imprisonment under suspensory Act. Usual guards etc.
17th Lt-Col Reed V.C. GSO 27th Div. left for Mediterranean Force. Usual guards etc.
18th Nothing to report
19th Divine service
20th Bathing parade. Parades, Guards etc.
21st Received instructions regarding a School of bombs which was to be started with Capt H.S.S. Hilton-Green in charge. Coy employed on constructing suitable trenches and making magazines

magazine
(31st contd)
for divisional reserve of bombs.

22nd 1st class for instruction in bomb throwing was to arrive on 26th. All instructors were to be drawn from Cyclist Coy in the first place, and promising pupils were to be further instructed to assist in instruction.

23rd Improving on work for School of Bombs. Instructors arranged etc. Coy employed trench digging etc. Trench mortar party returned from trenches. Another sent in relief previously.

23rd Guards, working on School of Bombs, etc. Lt Otway on leave.

24th — do —

25th Fatigue parties despatched to MERVILLE for Canteen purposes. This party was to be sent regularly. Guards etc.

26th Arrival of parties from Bdes for instruction in Bomb-throwing. Parties were squadded and billeted.

27th Lieut Otway awarded Military Cross for work done in 2nd Battle of Ypres.
Instruction in bomb-throwing, parades etc.

28th Army workshop for making Trench Stores established at ARMENTIERES. Usual parades etc.

June
29th Work on Bomb-School, parades etc
30th — do —
31st 1 man slightly wounded by bomb explosion. Usual guards etc.

Army Form C. 2118.

# WAR DIARY or INTELLIGENCE SUMMARY.

**27 CYCLISTS**

July

1st Course of instruction in Bomb-throwing completed. Usual guards etc.

From 2nd to 10th
The usual work was carried out and everything reported satisfactory. Nothing to report excepting Usual Guards, Patrols etc.

11th Major-Genl Snow G.O.C. 27th Divn visited Bomb School and expressed his satisfaction with regard to work carried out in Bomb School.

12th Experiments with smoke-bombs – Infantry charge under cover of these bombs was found to be very satisfactory. Usual parades etc.

13th Usual parades etc guards etc: Lt Lyns proceeded on leave.

14th Water tested by Medical Officer found impure. Orders issued all water was to be boiled before drinking. Usual parades etc:

15th Inspection of Smoke Helmets by Medical Officer afterwards all helmets sprayed with solution. Usual parades etc

16th Nothing to report. Usual guards etc

17th Parades every morning with Smoke Helmets adjusted & usual guards etc.

18th As NCOs & men of this Company were drawn from different regiments a universal drill was brought into force. Usual Guards etc

18th Nothing to report. Usual parades guards etc

19th — do — — do —

20th Lt A'Kenny proceeded on leave. Usual parades. Improvements on bomb-school etc.

21st Usual routine. One man wounded by a bomb explosion.

22nd Sent party of NCO's & men for inoculation & usual routine.

23rd Usual parades. Another party sent for inoculation.

24th Bomb accident this day. No 4488 Rfn Smith of 4th RB killed & No 3776 Cpl Bent of 4th RB wounded. Usual routine otherwise

25th Usual routine. Nothing to report.

26th Lt Kenny returned from leave.

27th G.S. Officer 27th Divn inspected bomb school school. Usual guards etc

Army Form C. 2118.

# WAR DIARY
## or
## INTELLIGENCE SUMMARY.
*(Erase heading not required.)*

**27 CYCLISTS**

| Place | Date | Hour | Summary of Events and Information | Remarks and references to Appendices |
|---|---|---|---|---|
| | July | | | |
| | 28th | | Court of Enquiry ordered to enquire into cases of Rfn Smith (killed) & Cpl Brost wounded by bomb explosion. Usual routine. | |
| | 29th | | Nothing to report. Usual parades etc. | |
| | 30th | | Party for fatigue - wiring sent on this day and to be sent daily in future. Bridge guard, Billet guard & Parade for Company drill etc. | |
| | 31st | | Information received 5 francs valued at 3/8 English money. Nothing else to report. | |
| | 31st | | Usual routine - nothing to report. | |

August

1st  20 men under Lt Robinson paraded to report at CRE's office for instruction in making fascines. Usual parades etc.

2nd  Usual guards, parades etc

3rd  — do —

4th  Divine Services and guards etc.

5th  Scheme for infantry charge under cover of bomb throwers with smoke-bombs and men carrying French wire was carried out with satisfactory results.

6th  Nothing to report.

7th  Bathing parade + Physical exercise and usual duties.

8th  Usual Routine

9th  — do —

August

10th  Pte Darling of this Company slightly wounded by splinter of bomb 300 paces away from place of explosion. Usual parades etc.

11th  Lt Lynn & 50 men sent to unload barges loaded with coal. Usual parades etc.

12th  Pte Miles of this Coy awarded 28 days FP No1 by Court Martial. Sentence was read out on parade.

13th  Party for unloading coal sent again — usual parades etc.

14th  Usual guards, parades etc

15th )
16th )  — do —

17th  New course of Bomb Throwing lasting 8 days started this day. Usual parades etc.

18th  Usual guards etc

19th  Officer expert in catapult bomb-thrower visited bomb-school + gave demonstrations. Usual parades etc.

20th  Usual guards parades etc.

21st  — do —

22nd  Capt H.F.L. Stilton-Green proceeded on leave to England. Lieut Shafto assumed command

23rd  Sgt Hubbert + Pte Marriott of this Coy awarded 2 + 4th class medal of St George respectively. Usual parades etc

24th  Physical drill parade + working parties.

Army Form C. 2118.

# WAR DIARY
## or
## INTELLIGENCE SUMMARY.
*(Erase heading not required.)*

**27 CYCLISTS**

Instructions regarding War Diaries and Intelligence Summaries are contained in F.S. Regs., Part II. and the Staff Manual respectively. Title pages will be prepared in manuscript.

| Place | Date | Hour | Summary of Events and Information | Remarks and references to Appendices |
|---|---|---|---|---|
| | | | August | |
| | 25th | | Trenches received no inspn – rest myself | |
| | 26 | | about 10 Cyclist Companies. Guards etc. | |
| | 27 | | two extra working parties. Scouts to | |
| | | | 2 hour daily parties. sent out this day – | |
| | | | usual parades, guards &c | |
| | 28 | | All N.C.O. men employed on guards, | |
| | | | working parties etc – nothing to report | |
| | 29 | | Nothing to report. Usual guards. | |
| | 30 | | – do – | |
| | | | Lt. D.M. Kennedy of this Company admitted | |
| | | | to hospital suffering severely from sprained ankle – | |
| | | | & left knee – accident while riding | |
| | | | motor bicycle. Usual guards & working parties | |
| | 31st | | Capt Q.N.L. Wilson – began a week's leave | |
| | | | Usual Guards, parades etc. | |

Army Form C. 2118.

# WAR DIARY
## or
## INTELLIGENCE SUMMARY.   27 CYCLISTS

(Erase heading not required.)

September.

1st  Received news that Capt Shilton-Green was sick in hospital in England. Leave extended to 30th Sept 1915. Usual parades &

2nd Nothing to report.

3rd Work on Bomb School, parades, guards etc

4th Divine Service.

5th Published memos received regarding War Loan £37 worth bought by NCO's & men of this Coy. Usual parades etc.

6th Inspection of bicycles. All ranks warned

September warned

6th (contd) not to submerge cycle bearings in water. Usual parades etc.

7th Wiring party & party for instruction in Fascine making. Usual parades etc

8th Usual parades etc.

9th ——— do ———

10th Wiring party. Fascine making party and other working parties. guards + usual duties.

11th Received orders regarding move. Preparations made i.e. filling in trenches on Bomb School that would no longer be required. Usual duties.

12th Work on Bomb School etc Parades.

13th Winding up of Bomb School. Instructors returned to Units.

14th Inspection of bicycles to see if they were all in running order. Usual duties etc.

15th Handing over billets to 23rd Divl Cyclist Coy. Sent out advance party to report on road from here to destination. 23rd Divl Cyclists took over guards etc that were previously found by this Company.

16th Coy paraded at 9am, moved off at 10am. arrived MERRIS 1.30pm distance 10 kilometres.

17th Still at MERRIS waiting further orders

# WAR DIARY or INTELLIGENCE SUMMARY.

Army Form C. 2118.

**27 CYCLIST**

(Erase heading not required.)

September 1916

| Date | Summary of orders |
|---|---|
| 17th (Cont) | regarding move. |
| | Bn paraded at 10am to walk to THENNES arrived there about 1.30pm distance about 20 kilometres. Entrained 11pm/12 about midnight |
| 18th | Arrived at LONGUEAU at 9 am. detrained ready to move off at 9.30 am. Move off to further end of village and started cycle in good Road orders but Company was no good again at start and was not to go Officers despair knew in which went direction. Passed at DOURS and moved on —— roads very hilly — arrived Longpré at 5 pm distance 19 kilometres. Billeted outside village at went in to get drinks. Later Company Billeted in farm. |
| 19th | Paraded at 9 am. and arrived at destination BELLEIVAL on main road near VIGNACOURT the road between going from ABBEVILLE to DOULLENS. Bn surrounded by nine acres. At Quebec near mt. Preparations commenced for making Bomb School. Usual parades. |
| 22nd | 1st Platoon employed together with RE's in making Bomb proof dug out to hold the Div Reserve of Bombs. Remainder of |

| | |
|---|---|
| | Company — parades, working parties etc. |
| 22nd | Went to Corps School. Parades etc |
| 23rd | Instructors for Bomb School arrived Usual parades etc. |
| 24th | Parties detailed for instruction, work connected with Bomb School. 1st class of Cyclist Coy Received their morning with men under instruction in Bombs, Lewis gun, Physical Bayonet drill etc |
| 25th | Usual parades. 2nd platoon men to trenches with bench Mortar |
| 26th | Orders received to send 50 men to M.S. for Trench digging. The party was to set out daily for trench digging. |
| 27th | 1st Platoon and OC Coy Received reinforcement of No 3 platoon usual parades etc and set to relieve 1st Batt Yorks |
| 28th | Control posts. |
| 29th | Usual parades. Usual working parties + duties. |
| 30th | Capt H.R.C. Hipton being struck off strength 4th Bn York & Lancs Regt to Head Qs. TF for duty etc arrived parades etc |
| 31st | Usual parades etc. |

## October

**1st** Physical drill as nothing to report. Res. Ok.

**2nd** The new "Kaiser" Boot Thick reinforced and special ribbed soles looking. 1 day only received on this day. Usual parades etc.

**3rd** Usual parades etc.

**4th** Working parties. School part returned. Usual parades.

**5th** Lieut. R/A Shafto Esmonde gazetted Captain this day. 2/Lt Cpn Bramwell arrived and assumed command of nos platoon. Lieut Anthrobus.

**6th** Inspection of quarters - helmets issued.

**7th** No distinct round heard about the bullet being very dreamy. NCOs were given extra remove map reading lectures & extra parades were arranged. Passes to outlying villages were allowed.

**8th** B.O.C. On usual orders that all men were to wear lights outside billets. Range.

**9th** Usual parade events. Aeroplane came down near the billet Plenty was sent to under arrangement if necessary - found that petrol tank had a shrapnel hole in it, this was eventually put right and the party was withdrawn.

**10th** Usual parades & guards.

**11th** Do.

---

## October

**12th** Party sent for fitting up latest turn. 1 man wounded took school lorries. Officer slightly wounded. Usual duties. Capt H.J. W. Dir-Green arrived - taken on strength and assumed command.

**13th** Usual work parades & guards.

**14th** Men parties sent out to take over control posts. Parades & usual duties.

**15th** Usual parades guards etc.

**16th** Party sent to inspect aeroplane that had brought down near fallen therein. to usual routine has carried out. Usual parades etc.

**18th** I forgot to make mention in the 1st but today a party that was sent to WARFUSÉE-ABANCOURT consisting of 1 NCO & men to establish a Post Post. The men had to conduct all drafts from this camp to where their Units were. This work was carried out very anticipatorily and as the various units in as district were spread out over a large area a party of cyclists for conducting purposes were found to be very handy indeed. The usual parades guards etc.

**19th** Usual parades etc.

**20th** All control parts guards found by 32nd Bn were to taken over by cyclist bn leaving Germany. Remainder of Bn paraded etc.

Army Form C. 2118.

# WAR DIARY
## or
## INTELLIGENCE SUMMARY.
(Erase heading not required.)

**27 CYCLISTS**

## October

**21st** Received order regarding move. All spare bombs, Stoves, and various articles returned to Ordnance Dump. Coy employed on cleaning up billets etc.

**22nd** Instructors of Bomb School returned to Units. Working party to R.E. Office.

**23rd** Coy paraded and moved off at 9:30am great difficulty was experienced on 1st part of march owing to so much traffic & infantry on the road. Eventually arrived PONT DE METZ about 2:30pm. Coy was billeted in large Rag factory. Coy allowed anywhere within the village but had to be in billets 8.0pm. Lights out 8.30pm.

**24th** Paraded at 2pm and proceeded to GUINEMICOURT where we arrived about 4:30pm. The road to this village was very heavy and up-hill nearly the whole way. Coy was billeted in large farm. Lieut Otway on leave.

**25th** Capt Shafto arrived from leave. Coy left the large farm mentioned in 24th & were billeted in various farms in the village. Route march & usual duties.

**26th** Usual parades & guards.

**27th** A map was prepared showing the Divisional area & posted up. Very strict orders were issued to the effect that no

## October

**27th (Contd)** one was to go outside this area. Usual Company duties.

**28th** Usual routine. Nothing to report.

**29th** do

**30th** Coy paraded under platoon Commanders & usual duties.

**31st** Boxes supplied with instructional set of Bombs from this Coy's stores. Usual parades.

# WAR DIARY
## or
## INTELLIGENCE SUMMARY.   27 CYCLISTS
(Erase heading not required.)

Army Form C. 2118.

Instructions regarding War Diaries and Intelligence Summaries are contained in F. S. Regs., Part II. and the Staff Manual respectively. Title pages will be prepared in manuscript.

| Place | Date | Hour | Summary of Events and Information | Remarks and references to Appendices |
|---|---|---|---|---|
| | | | November | |
| | | | 1st At [Aubigny] orders from [?]. Usual parades etc. | |
| | | | 2 Very heavy march. The roads were in a very bad state, so I omitted route marches in preference to physical and parades etc. | |
| | | | 3rd The new pattern belts [were] handed out to Durhams. This was the first information made for the next move. From information I think that our next move will be our own. Later confirmation have been received to the effect that all steps taken were previously suspended and postponed to the 16th inst. | |
| | | | 4th Usual parades, and went on parade for inst. All documents in the office | |

www.ingramcontent.com/pod-product-compliance
Lightning Source LLC
Chambersburg PA
CBHW081250170426
43191CB00037B/2101